First published 2024 by Burton Mayers Books
www.BurtonMayersBooks.com
Text copyright © Laura Payne
Illustration copyright © Laura Payne

ISBN 9781739367596

For my patients
It is a joy to know you all

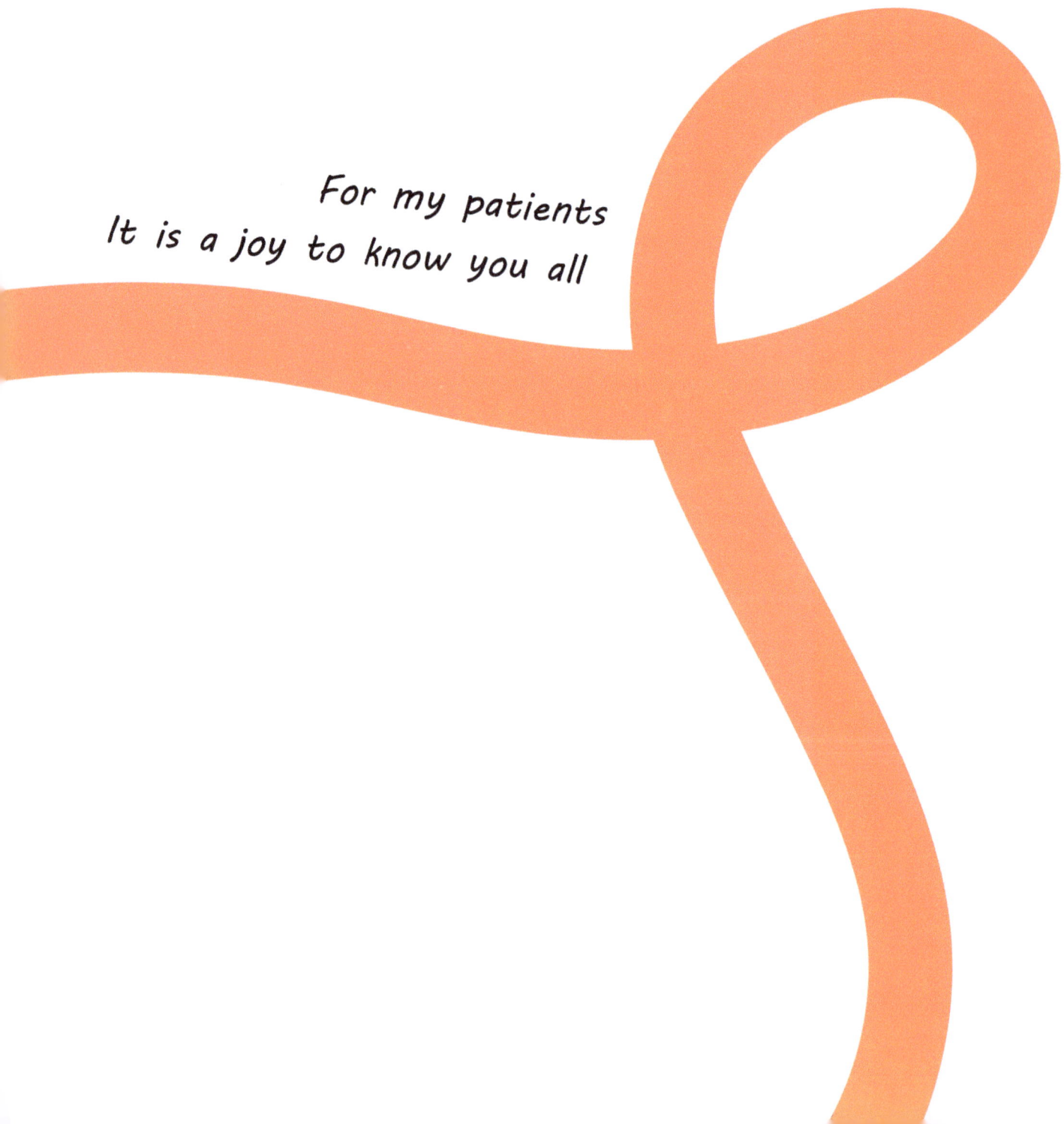

Ey up! Bonjour! Good morning!
Konnichiwa! Jambo!
A beaming smile, a little wave
How do you say "hello"?

Each of us is different
in the way we like to speak
It's one of the amazing things
that makes us all unique!

So let's all learn together!
Let's share and celebrate
the wonderful and varied ways
that we communicate!

I TALK LOUDLY!

I talk quietly.

I talk with a low voice.

I talk with a high voice.

It doesn't matter how we talk...

I use my tablet to talk.

I use my communication book.

I talk using my hands.

I sssstammer when
I t-t-talk.

It doesn't matter <u>how</u> we talk...

I talk quickly.

I... talk... slowly...

We all talk with different accents.

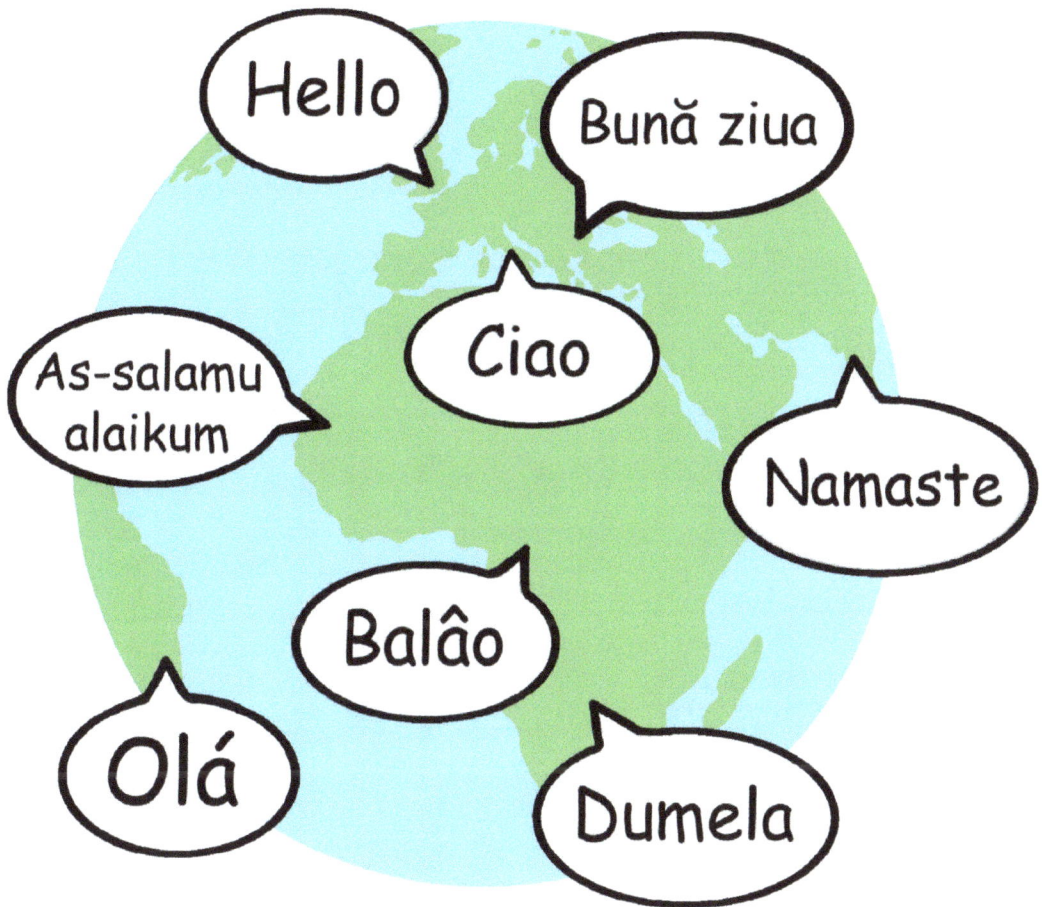

We all talk in different languages.

It doesn't matter how we talk...

It matters <u>what</u> we say!

I like talking lots
and lots (and lots!)

I find talking hard.

So make sure that you take notice

of every smile and sign and word

For we each have a story

and deserve to be heard

And we all share our message

in our own special way

It doesn't matter how we talk...

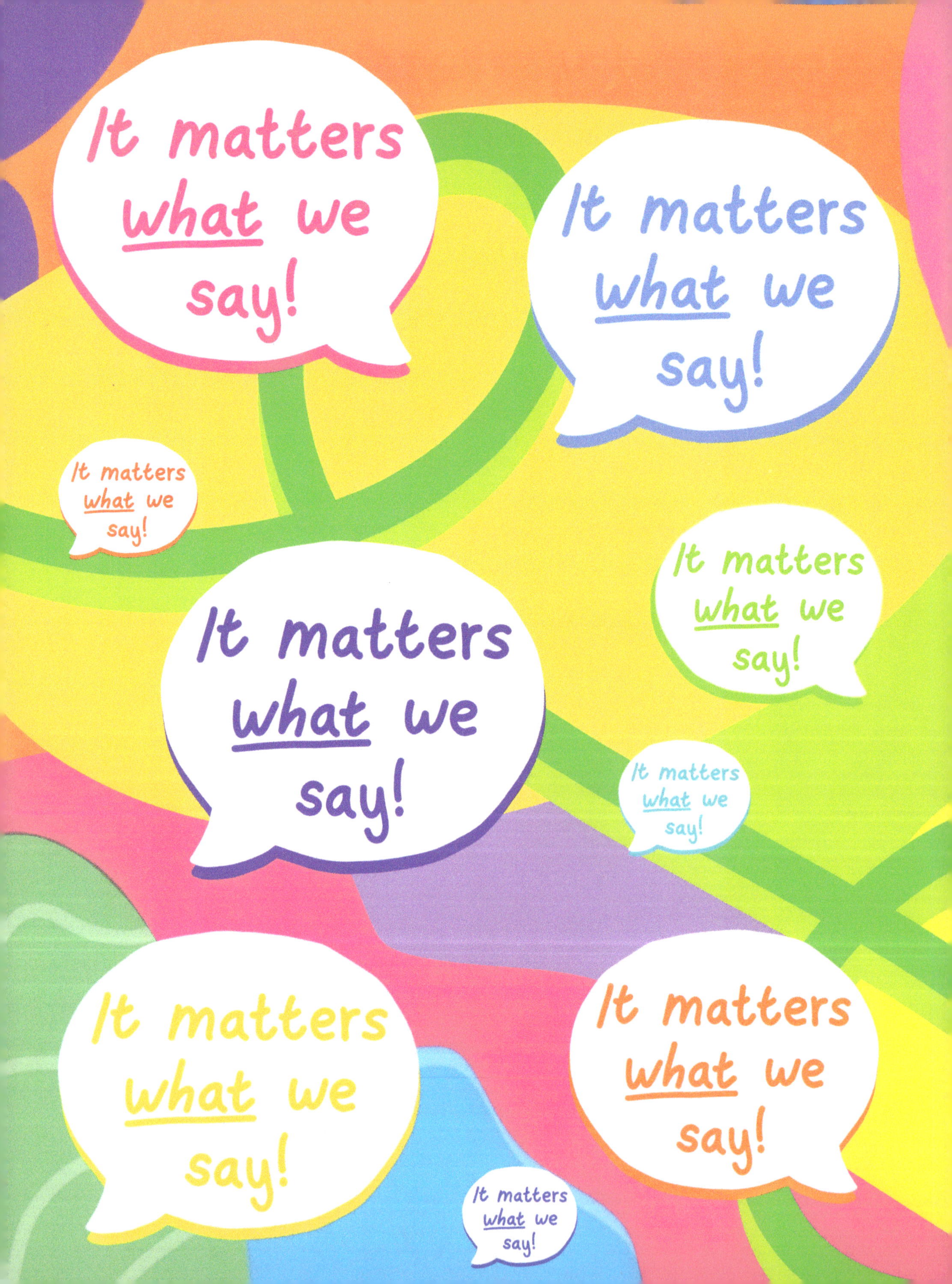

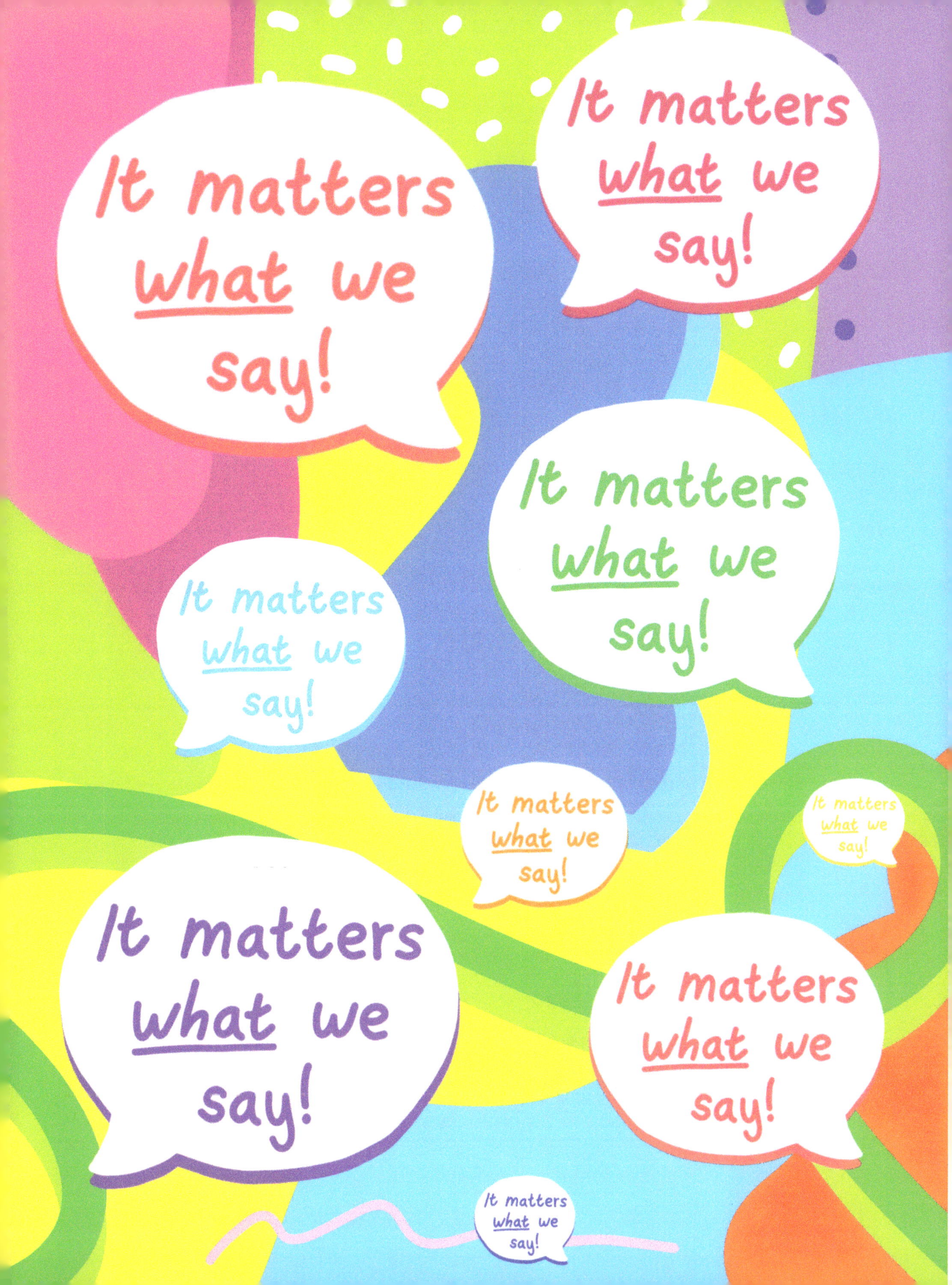

About the Author

Originally from the West Country, Laura now lives and works as a Speech and Language Therapist in South Yorkshire. Laura is passionate about communicative diversity and every person's right to have their voice heard and valued. In 2019, she received the Giving Voice award from the Royal College of Speech and Language Therapists for her disability activism. 'It Doesn't Matter How We Talk' is Laura's first book.

www.ingramcontent.com/pod-product-compliance
Lightning Source LLC
Chambersburg PA
CBHW041434040426
42452CB00020B/2971